NATIONAL
GEOGRAPHIC
School Publishing

A Bird Flies By

Marilyn Woolley

A bird flies by.
What bird is that?

That is a bald eagle.
It lives in the mountains.

A bird flies by.
What bird is that?

That is a snowy owl.
It lives in snowy places.

A bird flies by.
What bird is that?

That is a sparrow.
It lives in the city.

A bird flies by.
What bird is that?

That is a woodpecker.
It lives in the forest.

A bird flies by.
What bird is that?

That is a pelican.
It lives by the sea.